INSIDE THE MINDS OF
MEN

(WRITTEN FOR WOMEN...CONFIRMED BY MEN)

THE ASCOT AUTHOR

authorHOUSE®

AuthorHouse™
1663 Liberty Drive
Bloomington, IN 47403
www.authorhouse.com
Phone: 1-800-839-8640

First published by AuthorHouse   10/25/2011

ISBN: 978-1-4670-6729-4 (sc)
ISBN: 978-1-4670-6727-0 (ebk)

Library of Congress Control Number: 2011918723

Printed in the United States of America

CONTENTS

This book is dedicated to any woman who has been undeservingly put through hell while in a relationship with her man; yet still, she saw the benefit of keeping her faith, withstanding her struggles, not giving in to her own temptations and continued to live her life in a manner in which GOD was proud. Thank you so much for allowing the Light within you to shine, while so many others around you condemned you for it!

~ The Ascot Author~

PREFACE

Inside the Minds of Men (Written for Women . . . Confirmed by Men) is a compilation of over 1,000 men surveyed since 2009, throughout Western civilization, from ages twenty-five to fifty years old. My research has shown that the lessons shared throughout this book apply to most heterosexual men irrespective of race, color, political affiliation, financial income, educational level, or social status. Of all the men surveyed, each could agree that over 90 percent of the topics covered described him. Therefore, I find it probable that the lessons shared within this book apply to your man. This book will serve as a tool to enable a woman to better understand her man's behaviors and what makes him "tick" . . . all in an effort for her to avoid those unnecessary pitfalls that could lead to disappointment and undue heartache.

ACKNOWLEDGMENTS

I Send a Special Thanks to:

GOD Almighty; YOU are truly my Jehovah-Jirah! Because of YOUR Grace, I have everything I need and many of the things I want. YOUR Divine counsel has taught me that I am the owner of nothing . . . I am merely a steward of what YOU have given me. To whom much is given, much is also required; therefore, I humbly accept the calling that YOU have for my life. I will forever be indebted to YOU for the unconditional Love and Patience YOU showed me during my acts of foolishness when I chose to live outside of YOUR will.

Now Word Covenant Church in San Antonio, Texas, and the International Prayer Palace Church in Huntingdon, United Kingdom . . . your ministry was the spark that lit the flame that still burns in my heart today. Praise GOD, Praise GOD, Praise GOD!

My beautiful wife, Ms. Felicia (a.k.a. "2D") . . . not only is this book a dedication to you for your longsuffering;

it is also in honor of how you truly epitomize the essence of being a virtuous woman. Through it all, your spiritual strength has been unparalleled and it is a Blessing to share life's challenges and treasures with you. Thank you for "birthing" the potential you saw in me since day one. I am delighted to say that *my* accomplishments are *our* accomplishments, and I know that I'm only setting the stage for your women's ministry that you will soon share with the world!

Devin (Lil' DDK); Son, I am so proud to have you as my namesake. Words simply can't describe what you mean to me. As your father, it is an honor to have an active role in your life and I gladly accept the divine responsibility of raising you to become a respectable man.

My family and friends of my hometown, Pensacola, Florida. When all else failed, you have always prevailed. Thank you for all the love you show me every time I come back home to visit. No matter where life takes me, I will always take a piece of you with me.

The men and women of the US Armed Forces and their allies. Having personally served downrange during a time of war in our fight against terrorism, I understand what you and your families are going through. Thank you for your continued sacrifices while making such a difficult job seem so easy. It's a very large cost to cover the pricetag of Freedom . . . I salute you for the price you pay every day!

INTRODUCTION

"So the man gave names to all the livestock, the birds in the sky and all the wild animals. But for Adam no suitable helper was found. So God caused the man to fall into a deep sleep; and while he was sleeping, he took one of the man's ribs and then closed up the place with flesh. Then God made a woman from the rib He had taken out of the man, and He brought her to the man. The man said, 'This is now bone of my bones and flesh of my flesh; she shall be called 'woman,' for she was taken out of man.' That is why a man leaves his father and mother and is united to his wife, and they become one flesh."
(Genesis 2:20-24)

Before I begin, let me start by saying, "Thank You!" Thank you so much for allowing me the opportunity to share my depiction of what goes on inside the minds of men. In a world where "normal" seems to be the new abnormality with regards to a traditional loving relationship, I felt compelled to share the perspectives of men who still embrace a relatively old-fashioned point of view as it relates to the passage on the previous page. Through my experiences as a husband and a counselor, I am convinced that a successful, loving relationship with your spouse is not a "destination;" it's a never-ending journey. Just when you think you have gotten it all figured out, you are met with a new challenge that sometimes make you ask, *How in the world did I even get caught up with this man in the first place?* This is why it is important for a woman to examine her potential husband with her mind long before she decides to examine him with her heart (not to mention, her body). As adults, we are a direct reflection of our childhoods and upbringings. The joys, pains, insecurities, and inner conflicts we experienced throughout our childhood years are manifested into our adult lives. As a result, we wear "masks" to conceal our identities and even create facades to hide what's true. Finally, after years have gone by, our significant others get to see who we really are. Life has shown me countless examples of the effects on adults who grew up in either a predominantly loving family, an abusive family, or a single-parent family, and how different rearings ultimately shaped their adult behavior.

When a woman accepts a man's hand in marriage, she must understand that she's not only accepting his hand; she's also accepting the hands of all the people who have influenced him throughout his entire life up to the point of his proposal! Before saying "yes" to marriage, understand that you could be potentially saying "yes" to a number of unnecessary headaches you could have easily avoided had you taken the time to look. In fact, at least one of these "Five Headaches" come to mind:

1. *A Deadbeat Dad* . . . to me, there is hardly anything worse than a man who makes a conscious effort to not be involved in his child(ren)'s life! This is the type of guy who refuses to work a payroll job and chooses to work side-jobs and get paid "under the table" in order to keep from having to pay child support. All along, he disregards the reality of how his child now has to find other avenues to try to get an understanding of what a real man looks like.

2. *A man suffering from "Baby-Mama Drama"* . . . meaning you would have to deal with your man's ex-woman to whom he did not give a wedding ring; instead, he gave her at least three kids and then he decided to dump her and marry you! Chances are your man's "Baby Mama" might have a problem with that and resent you as a result, thereby making your life a living hell!

3. *A man who's financially irresponsible* . . . this is a man who spends his money as fast as he can earn it. Not to

mention, all the things that he spends his money on are for selfish gain (car enhancements, clothes, shoes, gambling, and other things to impress his so-called friends), while his household struggles to keep the utilities on and food in the pantry. Find out what your man's three-to-five year plan is, and if you find it to be a positive one, take notice as to whether or not he is actually carrying that plan out. If it turns out that your man does not have a plan (in other words, he's unable to articulate his life's goals and aspirations), that, too, could be a telltale sign that you may have to put in some serious work in order to be pleased with him overall.

4. *A man who doesn't work, doesn't want to work, is not making a positive contribution to the household, yet is always asking for your goodies* . . . if I have to explain this one, just start listening to your family and friends who already see that this bum is mooching off you and take their advice, at least this particular time, and do what's best for you, especially if you have children! Your children do not need to witness this type of behavior, because without proper guidance, a child could be easily influenced to believe that being with or becoming this type of man is okay. Now, granted, I understand economic crises will come; however, there is a lot to be said about a man who is willing to shovel shit, despite its smell, in order to provide for his family!

5. *A man who curses and disrespects his mother* . . . if he does not have a problem with cursing his mother out, what makes you think he would have a problem with cursing you out? Every man has a soft spot, and it usually begins with his love for his mom (or maternal guardian). If the guy you're dating has little to no regard for his mother, this is a crucial warning sign that you should not overlook. I will explain this one more as you read further into this book.

I once read a statement that said, "Men are attracted to women because of what they see and women are attracted to men because of what they hear; that's why women wear make-up and men tell lies!" I mentioned that passage to point out that, even if you cross-examine your man in the five particular categories mentioned above, there is still no guarantee you are going to avoid heartache; however, by taking into account what I've mentioned thus far, you would be surprised by how much of the "writing on the wall" will emerge from the simple questions you ask your potential male companion. Some important questions to ask a man can be about his childhood or how has he spent the last ten years of his life, because whether you believe it or not, we are all direct reflections of the past decisions we have made in life. In order to get the most sincere answer from a man when asking this type of question, it's going to have to take good timing on your part.

This isn't the type of question you'd ask your man while you two are on your way to dinner, because chances are he's in his mode to impress you; more than likely, he's going to tell you whatever it is he thinks you want to hear. It's also not a good time for you to ask him this type of question when he's angry, because his ego is soaring too high. One of the best times to ask a man the most personal questions is when he's feeling down or sad. For you to see your man sad means he's found a place or a state of mind within you where he feels comfortable and safe expressing this emotion. Of course he's not going to say, "I'm sad right now." It's going to take your keenest instincts as a woman to determine when that time is. Remember, your assessment of the answers he gives should be fair, and keep in mind that "Mr. Perfect" does not exist; however, with an open mind and intelligent approach, it is possible to find the perfect man for you!

I am clearly aware that many of the women reading this book are not married yet, but most have hopes of enjoying a promising, fulfilled marriage with that perfect match someday. If this is you, it is important that you *do not ask your man to marry you!* I realize societies are becoming more accepting of a woman who asks her man for his hand in marriage and feels that it is no big deal. However, my studies have shown that most women who proposed marriage either ended up divorced in less than five years or with a husband who made their marriage a living hell because he refused to do the right thing by way of marriage. With divorce rates being as high as they are anyway, a reasonable woman should not want to do anything to increase her chances of a failed marriage by asking a man to marry her. Besides, there's a good chance that if you have to ask him to marry you, his heart did not completely belong to you anyway. Even if and when he does ask you to marry him, ask him (with the kindest voice you have), "Sweetheart," (or whatever pet name you have for him), "Why do you want to marry me?" Don't get alarmed if he starts to stutter, because he probably won't expect you to ask such a question; he probably was thinking you'd be in "aww" by him asking the question in the first place. Nonetheless, be sure to look him in his eyes when he answers so you can measure the depth of his sincerity.

Enough about that for now; after all, this is only the introduction. However, it did not take me long at all before I could tell that there's too much information for me to share with you in just one book. You and I are either going to have to sit down and talk for a while or I am going to have to try to find more time to share with you what else I have learned about how we as men approach intimate relationships with women.

WHAT MADE ME DECIDE TO WRITE THIS BOOK?

I decided to write this book after attending a business conference in San Diego, California, where the women seemed to have been as beautiful as the city itself. While attending the conference, I recall three women seated at the same table as I who were holding a conversation about the things they did not seem to understand about their men. Since I was not trying to eavesdrop on their conversation, I started composing a text message in an attempt to avoid being included in whatever negative comments they had to say about men. That is when one of the women stopped and said to me, "Hey, you're a guy . . . what do you think it means when I have been dating my man for three months now and he won't invite me to his house and he only gives me his cell phone number and Facebook account to contact him?" I thought to myself, *Wow . . . is she for real?* Since I am a man who adheres to "The Male Code," I was not about to tell this young lady what I thought seemed to be blatantly obvious. So rather than violate the Code, I simply reiterated the story she shared with me, because even though her issue seemed open-and-shut to me, the truth of the matter was, I did not know her man. Therefore, I felt it would be wrong for me to speak emphatically about his behavior. After dissecting the woman's story and—slowly—replaying the scenarios that she shared with me, one of the other women sitting at the table said, "Girl, he's either married or has another woman!" I simply responded with, "Hey, those were your words . . . not mine." For the remainder of that week, I found myself answering "Why Do Men?" questions to a small group of women during almost every ten-minute break during the conference.

The next week, I was in Washington D.C. attending another conference, only to find myself engaged in a conversation very similar to the one I'd had in San Diego. To my surprise, I noticed that I had a captive audience of women who seemingly had a genuine interest in understanding where they had gone wrong in their relationships and what it would take to make them better. They sought to better understand what makes a man "tick" (i.e., what makes him feel content, happy, disrespected, annoyed, proud, sad, inadequate, and motivated when it comes to his relationship with his woman). After thinking back on my own experiences while in relationships with past girlfriends, always mindful to also include my current relationship with my wife, I explained the type of mindset I had as a single man versus the mindset I developed as a committed, married man.

Because the chat with those women regarding a man's approach to relationships went so well, many of them said, "Hey, you should write a book on this topic!" At first I thought, "No way!" then finally, I was then compelled to conduct a case study of over 1,000 heterosexual men throughout the United States and Northern Europe in an effort to bring readers the results of my findings that I share throughout this book. In order to comprehend the true intention of this book, you must read it as more than just words on paper and think of it as convenient reference tool for those times when you can't quite figure your man out. Hopefully by now you have settled into a comfortable chair and are ready to delve into what goes on *inside the minds of men*!

YOUR MAN IS SIMPLE

Okay, let's cut to the chase right from the beginning: if, by chance, you don't read another lesson in this book, I would suggest for you to read this one and become very familiar with it. Your man is a creature of habit who feels he is really not hard to please. Once he has found a method in life that works, it doesn't make sense for him to change. He strives to be a provider and protector, and he appreciates when he finds a woman who's confident and consistent with her behaviors, not one who's erratic with how she approaches a loving relationship with her man. Because of a man's simplicity, he doesn't respond very well to his woman when she displays helter-skelter behaviors. These types of behaviors mean that your man has a difficult time keeping up with you; you are riding the highs of life one minute and begin to argue or even cry with him in the next. He finds that type of behavior odd and sometimes irrational, and is usually left without a clue about knowing how to respond to you when you act that way. Your man responds positively to behaviors he feels are logical and will be quick to fulfill your desires when he feels they make sense. However, if he notices you go through some type of mood swing every other week or more often, then he will develop the mindset of "this woman is just crazy!" and he will look to avoid you in every way humanly possible until he feels you have calmed down and regained your senses.

In most cases, your man is willing to conform to your influences and become the man you would like him to be as long as it does not completely compromise who he is as a person. There were certain characteristics and qualities about your man that existed before you two even knew each another; therefore, it would be unfair for you to try to change him drastically from who he really is. The challenge, however, is for your man to clearly determine which of his characteristics are indeed desirable qualities and which of his characteristics are detrimental behaviors for the woman he's in a relationship with—you. Some men fall victim to self-sabotage, which happens when a man is not used to a good thing and may intentionally try to disrupt his happiness with you in order to regain a sense of normalcy. This type of man is mentally twisted and needs to be carefully examined before a woman considers having a serious commitment with him.

As for your man, he does not require too much from you as long as you reference what I call a man's "R.F.L. Theory."

The "R" stands for *Respect* your man; ironically enough, this male expectation seems to come as a surprise to more women than I initially would have thought. A working definition for respect is "for one to be esteemed, highly regarded, admired, reverenced, shown deference, and honored." When it comes to a man's order of importance, he would rather be respected by you before he's loved by you. Think about it. When was the last time your man insisted that you needed to love him? Chances are, it's been a while, if at all. If your man is insisting that you must love him, that's a pretty clear sign that he is dealing with issues of insecurity. Now, when was the last time your man insisted for you to respect him or mentioned that he felt you disrespected him? I'm sure you won't have to take nearly as long to answer my second question versus answering my first. Respect is almost as important to your man as breathing is; this became a personal requirement for your man when he began watching the men whom he admired at an early age. Every male your man has ever admired or wanted to be like had a following of people who esteemed him and/or humbled themselves as a result of the high regard they had for him because of his position or title, as evidenced in the way most people treat a man who is the pastor of a church, the CEO of a business, a commander in the military, the kingpin of a gang, or holds some other position of authority. Even if your man does not wear any of these titles, there is still something that exists within or about him which he feels is worthy of others' respect. When it comes to his woman, a man holds her to a higher standard than he does others when it comes to him being respected. Your man's rationale is that out of all the people in the world, he should have you in his corner to rely on. Your man feels that, because he is oftentimes slapped with the trials and ridicules of life outside of his home, the last person he should have to compete with in a contemptuous manner, on a regular basis, is his woman. Your man wants to be your protector and problem solver, and usually takes this responsibility very seriously. By doing so, the last thing in the world he wants to feel is that the person whom he's laying his life on the line to protect is disrespecting him. Your man holds you to a higher account to respect him, and this feeling is generally fueled by the fact that he cares about you more than anyone else.

Your man wants to be viewed as the king of his castle (even if only in his own mind), and he likes the opportunity to fix his woman's problems during her time of need. Your man does not like it when you consult another man to fix a problem before granting him the opportunity to do so first, or even if that other man is your father. Given the situation, sometimes it's best to make your man feel as if he has fixed your problem even when you have known all along that it was actually you who guided the fix. Please understand that I am not encouraging you to lie to your man; I'm only encouraging you to use that mysterious sixth sense you have developed as a woman and strategically guide your man in the direction you want him to go and make him feel like he's fixing your problem. If you are asking yourself, *What's this mysterious sixth sense he's talking about?* then perhaps you have not developed this ability yet. I've said it before and I'll say it again, "God put something special in women that He didn't put in men." If you know what I'm talking about, you understand that for you to master the ability to make your man think he's in control of "fixing your problem" is somewhat of an art form, he can't be aware of what you're doing. Because your man is no dummy (I hope), you may have to work at mastering your sixth sense for a while until the art of performing it becomes instinctive to you.

Disrespect has many different faces and multiple levels, and it oftentimes can only be described by your man as what it actually looks like to him. Unfortunately for women, men are usually reactive when it comes to expressing that they feel a woman has disrespected them. You could ask your man to name the things he feels would be considered disrespectful for his woman to do in an attempt for you to ensure you don't cross those lines, and after he cross-examines your motives for even asking such a question and feels comfortable with responding, your man may entertain the topic and attempt to name the ways in which he would feel disrespected. Even then, your man will not provide you with an all-inclusive list of things that he considers disrespectful, mainly because he won't be able to think of them all. For this reason, experience will have to be your best teacher.

The "F" stands for *Feed your man*. As the old saying goes, "One of the best ways to a man's heart is through his stomach." Men love women who can cook. Whether prehistoric or not, men still love the idea of coming home to a hot, home-cooked meal, even if your work day was just as long as his. Of course, a good man will take into consideration his woman's work schedule and make the necessary adjustments, perhaps grabbing some takeout or cooking a meal himself, and not try to obligate her to cooking a hot meal every night. In case you were wondering, your man would like for you to prepare him a good, home-cooked meal at least twice a week. To him, he feels cooking is a way for you to show your love and appreciation for him. This feeling of love and appreciation a man gets from his woman preparing a meal for him goes way beyond his individual nature, it goes back to what he has come to know as being part of his culture. Since the evolution of a more contemporary lifestyle, your man has had to conform to a household that's less traditional where the expectation for his woman to cook him a meal is not as demanding. Nevertheless, he still appreciates when you take the time to prepare good food. A good way for you to mellow your man's mood is to prepare his favorite dishes the way he likes them about every other week. Your sincere efforts will make him find you hard to resist.

The "L" stands for *Love your man*. Men love to be loved; when a "good" man sees and feels that his woman loves him for who he is and not for what he may have, it compels him to be more pleasing to her. Most men will not reveal the fact that they're completely in love with a woman until she has done so first. This is usually because they do not want to risk exposing this intimate emotion until the woman has voiced and confirmed that she feels the same way. This is mainly because men have trust issues. It takes far longer for a woman to gain her man's trust than it takes for her to lose it. However, if he has expressed to you that he loves you before you have, although this is rare, there's still a good chance that he's sincere. Like I said before, take time to notice your man's eyes whenever he says, "I love you," because the eyes don't lie! Of course there are always exceptions to every rule, but rarely will you find a man who has trained his eyes to lie just as well as his mouth.

YOUR MAN IS VISUAL

Although a woman's attraction to a man may oftentimes begin because of what she sees from the inside out, a man's attraction to a woman is typically driven by what he sees from the outside in. Men are very shallow and have a difficult time embracing a woman's worth if they are not attracted to how she looks in the beginning. Whether she's big, small, skinny, fat, light dark, tall, or short—there are men in this world who love each type. Yet, the point I'm making is that before a man will even consider a woman to be a worthy candidate for a relationship, he must first be attracted to her based on how she looks, because he's extremely visual and loves some eye candy. In fact, over 90 percent of the men I surveyed confirmed that it was the physical attraction he had for his woman that motivated him to even consider finding out what she was about. It's not that a woman has to look like some type of celebrity, actress, or supermodel; she just has to have some type of physical quality about her that he finds attractive. Speaking of celebrity actresses, did you know that most men created a "Celebrity-Girlfriend List" while they were growing up as young boys? In case you didn't know, a Celebrity-Girlfriend List is a list of celebrity actresses that boys create to identify the women they have as fantasy girlfriends. This celebrity girlfriend selection is very similar to how kids used to say "Bingo!" whenever they saw a nice car they liked or or "Punch Buggy!" whenever they saw a Volkswagen car while on the highway taking a family trip. More often than not, the Celebrity-Girlfriend List was a mental list of names that boys kept to share and compare with their other male friends. As strange as it may seem, over 80 percent of the men I surveyed admitted to actually writing their Celebrity-Girlfriend List down on paper and keeping it in their school notebooks or writing celebrity names on their bedroom wall (did I mention that men were simple?).

Personally, I still remember when I was approximately six years old and I created my own top ten Celebrity-Girlfriend List. In fact, allow me to take a walk back down memory lane and share my list with you. My list consisted of (1) Linda Carter as Wonder Woman; (2) Bernadette Stanis as Thelma on the 1970s television sitcom *Goodtimes;* (3) Dawn Wells as Mary Ann on the sitcom *Gilligan's Island*—although Ginger, played by actress Tina Louise, was a hottie on that show, Mary Ann displayed a "girl next door" demeanor, which suggested she may have been more nurturing (a quality that men find hard to resist); (4) Janet Jackson as Charlene on the 1980s sitcom *Diff'rent Strokes;* (5) Catherine Bach as Daisy Duke on the 1980s television program *The Dukes of Hazzard;* (6) 1980s CBS sportscaster and actress Jayne Kennedy; (7) Heather Thomas as Jody Banks on the 1980s television show *The Fall Guy;* (8) model and actress Beverly Johnson; (9) all three main actresses on the 1970s show *Charlie's Angels*; and (10) Phylicia Allen as Clair Huxtable on the 1980s-90s sitcom *The Cosby Show*. This type of list is usually no longer kept by the time a boy reaches puberty, because that is (usually) when his innocent thoughts of a simple crush on women are normally replaced with perverted ones. Even in adulthood, your man keeps (at a minimum) a mental Rolodex of the celebrity women whom he tastefully admires; perhaps I will share my modern-day celebrity list when I see you!

Ironically, over 80 percent of the men surveyed did not particularly care to see their woman as eye candy, because they know how most men are . . . like them! Have you ever seen a dog who has found himself in an unfamiliar area (i.e., a new backyard, outdoor park, etc.) and suddenly sniffs the area and begins to periodically pee on nearby trees, shrubs, the fence, or even on the ground? This peeing gesture symbolizes the dog is marking his territory, thereby sending the message "This territory is mine." The same could be said about a man who notices a large number of male onlookers who are noticeably eyeing his woman in a public setting. The man will want to send to the other men the message "Hey, she is mine, and I am stating my claim on her, right now!" I am not subscribing to the rhetoric that all men are dogs; this is simply my humanistic way to describe a man peeing on his tree, so to speak. So if and when you notice that your man becomes a little more affectionate and attuned to your needs when you two are in a predominately male public setting, be flattered by the message he is trying to send others: "This is mine . . . she's with me!"

Your man loves for you to have a clean, well-maintained appearance that does not look as if you had to spend your (or his) entire paycheck to look that way. At certain times *most* men see their woman as their "trophy," or, better yet, a representation of themselves. So in your man's absence while you're at work, church, shopping, exercising, or at the soccer game, he would like for others to see you and think, "Man, [Place your man's name here] has a very nice-looking, respectable woman; he's got him a good one."

As for a man who's on the dating scene looking for "Mrs. Right": not only does he look for a beautifully maintained woman; he looks for a woman who has traits similar to his mother's. This is exceptionally true if the man grew up as a "momma's boy." Remember earlier when I chose Mary Ann over Ginger? That's because not only was Mary Ann beautiful but she also possessed a nurturing quality similar to a mother's, whereas Ginger, who was also beautiful, possessed more of a selfish trait and seemed to be more interested in her own personal gain than that of others. Any man who had a close relationship with his mother while growing up usually wants to find a spouse who possesses those nurturing qualities his mother had, because he views that quality as a place of refuge whenever his heart needs consoling. Most times your man simply needs a kind, encouraging word from you during those times when things didn't go well at his job, when he was betrayed by a friend, or even when he hurt himself after participating in athletics—similar to what his mom used to do. Do not misconstrue the fact that your man is not looking for you to be his mother; it's just that he looks for a nurturing quality within you to help him during those times when he's feeling vulnerable.

In many cases the term "momma's boy" has been used with a negative connotation; that is not the case here. Think of the term "momma's boy" as describing that little boy who developed a loving, respectful bond with his mother at a very young age and, as he grew into adulthood, still adhered to many of her teachings and would do anything to protect his mom no matter the cost. If the qualities I've just listed describe a momma's boy in your mind, then I am guilty as charged. I have found that some people equate the term "momma's boy" with the terms I use, such as "big baby," "adult child," "spoiled rotten," or a "lazy-ass man." This type of irresponsible man walks around with a chip on his shoulder and acts as if the world owes him something. He is used to getting anything and everything from his mother or maternal guardian and likely had that kind of mother who prepared his plate and placed it on the table for him, washed and folded his clothes, gave him money without requiring an incentive for him to earn it, and, lastly, made excuses for him and turned a blind eye and deaf ear to fact that she was crippling an able-bodied man before passing him on to a woman who is left with the challenge of correcting the irresponsible behaviors of a man who's mom continued to feed him through an umbilical cord which she refused to cut!

I guess I got a little passionate about this particular subject because I know too many mothers who overly coddle their teenage sons, but do not acknowledge the fact that someday their little boy will soon need to become a responsible man. There are very few cases where a immature boy becomes a responsible man overnight, so it is important to for mothers to find a proper balance in embracing the little boy of today while grooming him to be a responsible man for tomorrow. Who knows, you could very well be the woman who has ended up with a man whose mom coddled him long after his coddling expiration date has passed.

YOUR MAN IS SEXUAL

Isn't good sex a beautiful thing? It's ironic is that a lot of women don't even know what good sex is. Have you ever found yourself in a situation when you thought the sex you were having with one guy was so good, but after getting with a new guy, you realized the sex you were having with that last guy wasn't what you had psyched it up to be? Good sex is experienced when the chemistry between a man and woman makes them connect intimately on mental, emotional, and physical levels that put them in rhythm, in sync, and allow them to harmoniously become one. When these sexual essentials come to life in the manner in which nature intended, the experience can be heavenly! It usually takes time for a couple to develop such chemistry, because in the beginning of most "sexcapades," you and your man usually have different agendas. As for a man, before he can reach that "heavenly plateau" of giving a good sexual experience to his woman, he must first go through his selfish phase (*At least I got mine!*). Personally, I consider this to be a learning curve men go through, and some men happen to have a steeper learning curve than others.

Have you ever taken the time to think of the seriousness involved when deciding to have sex? First of all, let's think of the traditional (some call it missionary) position in which sex is performed. A woman lying on her back with her legs up in the air in a "v" or "u" shape is one of the most vulnerable positions known to man. When a woman assumes this position, she is essentially saying, "I trust you and willingly submit myself to you, and I am ready to receive whatever you may have for my body right now." Tell me, do you have a man in your life whom you feel is disciplined enough to accept that type of responsibility? Better yet, are you willing to make the conscious decision to give yourself to a man who has not completely proven himself to be worthy of your treasures? If so, be sure not to take him for granted! Secondly, when a man and woman become active sexually, they are never the same once the act is over. With each sexual encounter, a man takes something sacred from a woman's spiritual being after he has physically removed himself from her intimacies. All the while, he leaves something within her spiritual being that causes her to respond to him differently than she would have before the sexual act occurred (kinda' deep, huh?). Many problems occur when one of the two felt he or she connected with the other on all levels (mentally, emotionally, and physically), and the other person felt they only connected on a physical level. This is why it is impossible for two people to be the same internally. Long after they have left one another's presence, at least one of them is going to have an emotional or mental tie to the other as a result of the sexual experience they shared.

A man typically has sex for one of two reasons: for sexual fulfillment, or because he is in love. Fulfillment. It's been said that the only thing that separates human beings from animals is the fact that humans have a conscience, whereas animals do not. However, men, like most male animals, have sex to instinctively fulfill a need without necessarily discerning whom they have it with, just as long as the other member is a willing participant. Then there is love. In the midst of a man fulfilling his sexual needs, he eventually encounters a woman who has that total package he is looking for. Although the characteristics of the total package a man looks for when seeking a wife may vary, one of the main elements is being able to have great sex with her. Therefore, by the time your man decides to ask you to marry him, it's extremely likely that he has fallen in love with you. At this time, your man's desire to have sex with you is not only for the sake of his fulfillment; it's usually coupled with the fact that he's in love with you and wants to fulfill your sexual desires as well.

Whether married or unmarried, sexual temptations are difficult to withstand because they appeal to the normal and natural desires which nature intended. As told in 1 Corinthians 7: 3, "Marriage provides God's way to satisfy these natural sexual desires and to strengthen the partners against temptation. Married couples have the responsibility to care for each other; therefore, husbands and wives should not withhold themselves sexually from one another, but should fulfill each other's needs and desires."

Although I am one who believes the holy Bible makes for an excellent life manual and as a spiritual guide to help us successfully navigate through this not-so-simple world in which we live, I also believe our Creator has blessed each of His people with the logic and common sense to make sound decisions. I am saying this to emphasize the importance of adhering to your God-given conscience when upholding the passage I have quoted above from 1 Corinthians 7:3 I encourage all wives to use their spiritual abilities to decipher when it is appropriate for them to uphold their obligations to fulfill their husband's sexual needs and desires. I do not advise them to knowingly jeopardize their health following any infidelity just to keep the sanctity of their marriage intact. Because I am not partial to this belief, the same message applies to husbands who suspect their wives of placing them at risk because of sexual promiscuity; it is just that this book is written for women.

Your man appreciates quickies, especially unexpected ones. There are not too many things that exist in your man's life that can trump an unexpected quickie. It tickles him to pieces when his woman creatively offers him her "cookies." Whether it is in the dressing room of a department store or during halftime of the Super Bowl, your man appreciates unplanned sex. This was especially true for the younger men I surveyed. Although the same is true for the older men, I discovered that they appreciate a little more creativity in how the gift is presented, rather than just the thrill of spontaneity. As he gets older, your man begins to appreciate it more when you take the time to create a fantasy (i.e., wearing different hairstyles and colors, sexy lingerie, etc). Another example of sexual creativity is for you to talk sexy to your man in a dialect completely different from your usual voice—speak with a Spanish, Caribbean, French, British, or Swedish accent. This kind of activity adds spice to the sex life of couples who have been together for ten years or more, and also enables men to have the opportunity to "tap" into one of their woman's different personalities (no pun intended).

If a man passes up spontaneous sex from his woman, it's usually for one of the following reasons: *(1) He's extremely stressed by money problems.* For example, one of the men I surveyed went from earning $96,000 per year at his job of 15 years, to being told that he had thirty days left at his place of employment before he would be released from the company and given a severance package that would pay him $1,200 per month for the next six months. He was a family man who had over $7,000 in monthly bills and expenses and less than $3,000 in savings. Do you think he was stressed? Absolutely!

(2) *His loved one is gravely ill.* This is a scenario that I can relate to personally. It was October 1999, in Oklahoma City, Oklahoma. I had just gotten paid; it was Friday afternoon and I was still riding the high of being a newlywed married for two months. After getting home from work, I walked over to the telephone and checked my voicemails, as it was my routine. One of the messages was from my cousin in Florida, informing me that my mother had suffered a stroke about two hours ago, the ambulance had just taken her to the hospital, and things were not looking good for her. After gathering my composure, I immediately booked a flight home that would get me to my mom's bedside by that evening. Once I arrived, my wife and I went straight to the hospital to see my mom. From late Friday night until Sunday afternoon, seemed like nothing else in the world mattered to me other than

spending my mother's last moments with her. My mother passed away later on that Sunday evening.

(3) *He's extremely tired.* One of the men I surveyed could truly relate to this example. He was a police officer who normally worked twelve-hour shifts and had been engaged to his fiancé for nearly three months. One day, while on duty, he and some of his fellow officers took part in a series of force protection police exercises that lasted for more than fourteen hours. Afterwards, the group participated in a mandatory physical fitness program that lasted for two hours. At the end of this exhausting sixteen-hour day, he came home to a fiancé who could not wait for him to indulge in her bag of "cookies," which she anxiously had waiting for him. The poor guy told me that he didn't even have the energy to eat dinner, not to mention the "cookies" that his fiancé had to offer. So, he declined her offer, collapsed on the bed, and went straight to sleep, leaving his fiancé hot and bothered with thoughts of whether or not he had possibly been cheating on her.

The point I look to make is, although these circumstances are rare, they can occur. A woman must understand that any of the circumstances described in these three examples will indeed trump her man's desire to have a quickie.

Ever wondered why your man typically falls asleep after sex? Although I am not a doctor, I have learned that, according to a study conducted by New York University's science, health and environmental reporting program, during ejaculation, men release a cocktail of brain chemicals, including oxytocin and the hormone prolactin. The release of prolactin is linked to the feeling of sexual satisfaction, and it also determines the "recovery time" of men; in other words, the time your man must wait after ejaculation before going another round. Studies have shown that men with less prolactin have faster recovery times. Therefore, the older your man gets, the more prolactin he produces, resulting in the hormones released during an orgasm to cause him to feel sleepy. Speaking of aging, the older your man gets, the more he loses his libido, the energy and desire that motivates his sex drive. Most men are not aware of when their libidos begin to decrease, and as a defensive measure, some men will begin to make excuses for not being able to go another round, saying things like "give me a minute," "it's been a long day," or "it's not you, it's me", when the reality is simply that he is succumbing to a natural, normal part of the aging process.

YOUR MAN IS SELFISH

Your man is selfish, whether consciously or unconsciously, and oftentimes he takes you for granted. Sometimes a woman becomes so efficient at taking care of her man's needs that his behavior may begin to appear as though he is unappreciative of her attention to detail. This is not to say that he is ungrateful; it is more likely that he is simply forgetting to express his gratitude for your many acts of kindness.

Be careful not to give your man too much credit when it comes to knowing your specific needs. If you do this, you could possibly be creating self-induced headaches or heartaches for yourself when you make one or all of the top three statements at some point in time: "We've been <u>dating/married</u> for [insert number here] years, he should just know that about me by now," or "I thought every man his age knew how to do that." Just because your previous man knew how to do "that" does not mean that your current man does. (I'll let you fill in whatever "that" is.) The other statement to avoid is, "He isn't dumb; he should be able to read between the lines." In reality, he may very well be dumb to your specific needs. In order to ensure that you and your man are on the same page when it comes to your specific desires, sometimes you may have to make it plain to him and spell things out before he actually understands what it is you're looking for. By this time you may have become extremely frustrated with your man and want to curse his dumb ass out for not being able to read between your lines. However, it's key for you to remember to not be disrespectful when you are explaining your wishes to him (remember the "R" in my R.F.L. theory).

If it has been determined that your man is consciously being selfish toward your specific needs; if it's within his means to fulfill your requests, but he has literally told you he is not going to honor your desires, then this should be all the information you need in order to make a sound decision about this particular aspect of your relationship with him. By saying this, I am not suggesting for you to divorce or break up with your man; nor am I suggesting that this is a green light for you to go out and disrespect him. All I'm saying is now that you know where your man stands concerning this particular issue, you are now left with the challenge of discovering the best way to get through to him and expressing how important it is for him to fulfill your specific desires.

For the women who have been dating their men for awhile, yearning for their relationship with him to go to that "next level" and asking themselves, *I wonder when is he going to ask me to marry him?,* please understand that the likelihood of your man asking you to marry him significantly decreases when you are already providing him with everything that comes along with a marriage anyway. There are so many women who just go about it the wrong way when it comes to getting a man worthy of the love she has to give. Then she ends up giving her love to a guy who doesn't even come close to showing her the same type of love in return.

YOUR MAN LIVES BY A DOUBLE STANDARD!

A man can be extremely critical of your cleanliness or the lack thereof, and this is especially true during the dating phase. If and when he notices you do not keep your personal appearance and living conditions tidy, i.e., if he visits your home, uses your bathroom, and discovers hair on the baseboards or on the back of the toilet seat, skid marks in your toilet (not to mention skid marks in the underwear you accidentally left on the floor), seeing this will definitely give him a negative connotation in his mind regarding your cleanliness. As a result, he will be far less compelled to eat your food and go the extra mile with you toward a meaningful relationship. However, if he himself displays those same characteristics, your man expects for you to grant him a "pass" regarding these particular shortcomings and be more understanding, as well as supportive of him while encouraging him to do better . . . because to him, that's just part of being a man.

WHY DO MEN CHEAT?

I have had a number of women ask me the question, "What makes a man cheat on his woman?" To me, that's an age-old question that does not seem to get better with time. Nonetheless, I will give three answers to this question for you to ponder.

(1) *It's in his genetics.* Many centuries ago, before laws and civilization were in place, men were charged with the duty of populating their villages, towns, and ultimately the world, with people to inhabit the land. As cultures began to slowly develop, the poor, lower classes were intentionally joined with one another by order of the majority leaders to produce able-bodied offspring to serve as field hands and cultivate farmlands, build buildings, discover medicines, and create new technology in order to have a functional society. All the while, the majority leaders were not monogamous in their own marriages and oftentimes would have relations with their subordinate help, sometimes having children together during the course of their inequities. This went on for hundreds of years before ethics were adhered to and laws were put into place forbidding these types of behaviors. Unfortunately, because these unethical behaviors ran rampant for so long, it became an involuntary part of a man's being (i.e., it's in his

DNA), and I tell the women who as me that this is one reason why men cheat.

(2) *He's not compelled to do otherwise*. Women assume a great portion of the responsibility for male behavior. At no time is it appropriate or justifiable for a man grope and grab a woman simply because she may be wearing something that is too sexy or revealing. However, women need to understand that some men possess a Neanderthal trait that captivates his logic from time to time and causes him to do some ungodly things. The two greatest senses that a man responds to are sight and touch. When a man sees a woman he thinks is attractive, it's a serious challenge for him to not give any type of response whatsoever. He will either grunt, get wide-eyed, squint, do a double-take, sweat, or even get noticeably quiet in the presence of an attractive woman. Once his initial sense is aroused, he then hopes that his second strongest sense can soon be satisfied. And for heaven's sake, don't let the attraction be mutual between him and the other woman . . . that's usually where the sweating comes into place.

When a woman finds a man attractive and does her investigative research on him (you know what I'm talking about), finds out he's already in a relationship, and yet pursues him anyway, this is a relational foul on that woman's part. Then, to add further insult to what's quickly turning into a bad situation, the weak man who's already in a relationship yields to the other woman's temptation. This would not be the case if most women would agree to abstain from sexual relationships with men who are already spoken for. However, because there are so many women in the world who do not set respectable standards for themselves or their bodies, a man quickly develops the mindset of, *What one woman won't do, the next one will!*

If more women would take a stand to raise the bar on the level of respect they have for themselves and require from others, men would be forced to fall in line and conform to these higher standards. Most men will only work hard enough to reach the level of expectation that women have set for them. If a woman is only setting her standards of respect at a 3' level; the average man is only going to step up his level of effort to please her at a level of about 3'1". Very few men take the initiative to raise their level of respect for a woman to level five when she only requires his level of respect for her to be at a three. However, if women would collectively raise their expectations to a level of 6' or better, men would have no choice but to fall in line and raise their levels of respect in order to meet those standards. What I'm trying to say is, the sooner women figure out they have the ultimate influence on men's level of respect for them, the better off they will be. Because most women are not willing to raise their level of self-respect and continue to have sex with men who are already in relationships, this is another reason why men cheat.

(3) *He's Selfish.* Selfishness is *the* underlying reason why a man cheats on his woman! A working definition for selfishness is: lacking consideration for others; concerned chiefly with one's own personal profit or pleasure. Think about it. Your man sees a woman, other than you, who he finds sexually attractive; in this case the woman has no idea that he's in a relationship with you. Out of your man's lack of consideration for: (1) God (the One he should ultimately be living for); (2) You, especially when you were under the impression that you and your man had made a vow, commitment, or pact to save your bodies for each other; (3) His children, i.e., he disregarded or failed to count up the costs involved in his children being caught up in a messy divorce or custody battle and runs the risk of losing them from his life forever; (4) Himself—he knows that sex always feels better without a condom, so he rolls the dice and goes in unprotected for a quick five or six strokes, yet this time he rolls "snake eyes" when he discovers that he contracted a deadly sexually transmitted disease.

A man is so driven by the sense of sight that it will make him compromise his values if he's not careful and fails to surround himself around positive influences. It's important for a man to set his sights on things greater than his own selfish sexual pleasures and be prepared for the times when he'll come face-to-face with sexual temptations from the women I described in Answer # 2. This is why I have found refuge in Proverbs; chapters 5 and 7, because it was God's grace that kept me protected during my acts of selfishness.

YOUR MAN IS PRIDEFUL

Ever notice how your man is usually reluctant to go to the doctor when he hurts himself or is feeling sick? Or perhaps you wonder why it takes him so long to finally admit when he's in pain? It's all because your man is very prideful and possesses a macho trait that emerges more frequently than you probably realize. Far too often, your man avoids sharing his true feelings with you because he does not want to present himself in a manner that would cause him to look weak. This mentality has been deeply instilled in him. For years, men have been told not to show their deepest vulnerabilities and emotions; doing so would leave them having to prove themselves as being capable of fitting in with the rest of their male peers. In fact, men instinctively bought into this mentality so much until women began to feel the same way about how men should act. For instance, what does a real man look like to you, and what are his traits and characteristics? More than likely, your answer will reflect traits and characteristics of a man who is strong, loves sports, and is a protector who provides for his woman. By-and-large, those are often the same answers most men would give. However, this type of expectation from women and society makes it difficult for men to expose their softer side. In fact, I will speak more about this particular point later.

Because of your man's pride, he is also very competitive; he unconsciously sizes up other men just to see how he thinks he compares. Even when it comes to a simple handshake, men learn a lot about each other's level of masculinity, to include his athleticism by the way they shake each other's hand. It's not that all men like sports, I'm just saying that anything your man takes pride in doing, he does it competitively. Rest assured that there's something your man feels he's one of the best at. i.e., best doctor, lawyer, truck driver, graphic designer, computer technology wizard—you name it. This inner confidence stems from how your man was mentally and psychologically programed at a very young age. Whether it was learned from family, the media, society, or all of the above, most men feel that more pressure was placed on them to be the best or to be winners rather when compared to the pressure placed on girls. In fact, a lot of times, the prize that boys would get for being the best or coming in first place would be "The Pretty Girl." Very few people take interest in the man who comes in third, fourth or fifth place, so it didn't take too long for your man to figure out that he needed to be the best at whatever he took an interest in.

Your man has a pretty good idea of what type of men you consider good-looking or attractive; therefore, he tries to do things to be equally as appealing to you. A man loves to receive a good report card from his woman. Be sure to stroke your man's ego whenever and wherever feasible, because men unconsciously gravitate towards wherever his masculinity is fed. However, only stroke his ego when you're being sincere; otherwise, this would not do either of you any good. *Do not* tell your man he is hot when you know he's not even warm (even when he thinks he's doing his best work); otherwise he would not be compelled to change and would just continue to do that same annoying thing he does that you may have once implied you liked or enjoyed. Although your man appreciates your flattery, he would much rather you be honest with him instead.

Going back to the pride issue, be sure to uplift your man whenever and wherever feasible. Your man appreciates hearing an occasional second-hand compliment you have paid him in his absence. When your man learns of such compliments you have given him, it makes him feel appreciated that his efforts have been validated through your testimony, and he will be inclined to make an attempt to earn your public praise again (I've already told you . . . men are simple). However, be careful of the type of compliments you give your man in his absence; especially to other women, because you may find yourself having to put your female friends in check for trying to find out for themselves how good your man really is—you know what I'm talking about!

A woman should also be mindful of how well or how often she pays a compliment to another man, especially when she's with her own man. As long as it is within good taste, typically a man will not have a major problem accepting his woman paying another guy a compliment. In case you were wondering, two is usually the maximum number of compliments you can pay another guy in the presence of your man before you begin to see your "prideful" man reveal his discontentment with your willingness to praise someone other than him. If, or when, he feels the gleam in your eyes is potentially being caused by another man, more than likely he will become upset with you. This definitely holds true if you talk about your previous boyfriend or husband. Do not voluntarily share any special qualities about previous relationships with your current man. Bottom line, your man does not want to hear it, because that type of discussion just says to him that you are admitting you miss your previous man and wish you could still be with him. Needless to say, with pride often comes insecurity.

Also, your man does not want you to overly remind him about his previous relationships with other women. Face it: he knows what went on in those relationships better than you. So if your man feels you harp on his past too much, you can rest assured that you are depriving yourself of an undiscovered portion of his love because of your unwillingness to let the past go. Your man would love nothing more than to start anew and have the fair chance of creating memorable moments with you. One of the best ways a man feels he can make a memorable moment with his woman is through creating a child. Although most men are not always eager to procreate initially, whenever he determines he's ready to have a child, you can bet your last dollar that he wants to have a son. For a man, to have a son not only allows him to have someone to carry on his name, he also feels it gives him a chance to have a replica of him whom he can live vicariously through. There's a yearning that dwells inside most men to have a son they can play sports with, go to the barbershop with, fart with, and teach and provide him with mentoring that will help him become a successful young man. As sons get older, fathers look forward to things like playing golf, going fishing, watching sports games, and going over to their son's house after he becomes an adult.

This does not mean your man does not value the gift of having a daughter, because he can do nearly all the things I've mentioned with his little girl. However, if your man never has a son, he would be left with the challenge of suppressing the wishes of having a biological namesake. To him, a son makes his legacy complete.

HE WANTS A SMART, INDEPENDENT WOMAN

Do you feel your man finds your success to be intimidating and he is reluctant to fully support you as a result? If so, I encourage you to consider reading Proverbs 31:10-31, in which a virtuous woman is regarded as someone who is intelligent and business-minded; a woman who should be praised and celebrated by her man, not someone who gets dismissed by a man because of her accomplishments.

When it comes to a good man (i.e., one who is responsible and accountable for his actions), his intimidation has nothing to do with a woman's success and everything to do with her attitude. By default, a man first sees any adult female as a woman, but it is not until he has had time to examine her (usually in a matter of minutes) that he will not consider her worthy to be called a lady, or perhaps something less flattering. As I've already stated, a man considers any adult female to be a woman; however, his perspective of a lady is a peaceful, gentle woman who is confident and readily displays a nurturing quality and bears the fruit of a kind spirit that is humble, secure, and trusts God. A woman and a lady can experience the same type of heartache from a man and one will show outward displays of turbulent, obnoxious bitterness; while the other, although heartbroken, will confide in a good friend and channel her energies towards something positive and not blame her next man for the way she was treated by her ex.

Whether she is successful or not, most men can read the signs of a bitter woman from a mile away, so rather than feeling intimidated, most men simply elect to avoid the chore of trying to subdue the uninviting demeanor which some successful women have developed over time, thereby making it difficult for a man who is worthy of her love to achieve a legitimate breakthrough into her world. Once a man sees and feels negative energy from a woman, he is often left with the feeling of *Why should I even bother?* because more than likely, she is not willing to fall in line with the characteristics of a virtuous woman when assuming her role in a relationship. A good man's reluctance to commit to a meaningful relationship with a woman has more to do with her unyielding spirit to submit to him as her husband rather than her success and competence as a career woman.

Whoa, did I just say, "submit?" Yes I did. Now, what does submit mean to you? For me, it means one's willingness to conform to the will of another. As told by Ephesians 5:22-25, both men and women have the obligation to submit to one another in their relationships; in other words, a woman is charged with submitting to her man and her man is charged with submitting to the will of God. A man should love his woman enough to give his life for her; however, his woman's character and demeanor should be lovable enough for him to die for. Both men and women must accept that they have an enormous responsibility to one another in order to have a meaningful relationship, realizing that its importance goes well beyond their individual, oftentimes superficial successes.

Have you noticed how I have made emphasis on the term "good man?" I emphasize that point because I clearly understand that not all men are good—as a matter of fact, not being a good man is part of my own testimony.

Your man appreciates a smart and relatively independent woman; she doesn't have to have a college degree to win his love, she just has to have some street smarts, common sense, and be savvy. *Most* men appreciate a woman who wants to be with him but does not need to be with him. However, as a smart and intelligent woman, your man does not like it when you challenge or dispute even half of the decisions he make. Your man feels your wit and intelligence are meant to support him, not to undermine and frequently challenge him. Take time and analyze what you say to your man, and how you say it, because that could easily make the difference between a productive conversation and a terrible argument.

THE BEHAVIORS EVERY WOMAN SHOULD AVOID!

There are certain things that a woman simply should not do while in a relationship with her man. If and when she does one of the things that I'm about to identify, it will usually spell instant disaster. When reading this list, I trust you will not challenge the rules just because you think that your man is different and they will not apply to him. Try to avoid the temptation of allow these rules to be like saying, "Hey, here's a list of things to tick your man off whenever you feel the need to do so!" Because by doing so, he may get the last laugh. Without further ado, let me begin.

Do not:
(1) *Ask your man a question to which you feel you may not be ready to know the answer to.* Some women have the tendency to ask their man questions like, "Do you wanna go to the store with me?" then have the nerve to get upset if the answer is "no." There's no need for you to get upset with him for giving an honest answer. His response was a result of how you phrased the question: "Do you wanna go?" If you already knew you wanted him to go to the store with you, you should have said something like, "Honey, will you go to the store with me? I'd really appreciate it." By implementing this

simple change in your wording, it could save you a lot of undue stress with your man. This example was on a much lighter note than others I could have given, but nonetheless, it's still beneficial. Other types of questions you should not ask your man if you really don't want to know the answers include, "What are you thinking?" "Did you have sex with her? (*No*) But you wanted to, right?" "Are you still in love with her?" or the ever-popular "Does this make me look fat?" Just remember, if you're woman enough to ask the question, be woman enough to accept his answer.

(2) *Use his kid(s) as leverage in order for you to try to get what you want from him.* Not only will this make your man angry, it's an extremely insensitive way for a mother to show love and high regard for her own children. It's understandable to be angry or frustrated; however, it's important for you to understand that God holds the ultimate payback for your child's father, not you! Reference Romans 12:19 for the answer; afterwards, leave it in God's hands and don't be the reason why your kids don't get to spend time with their dad. Also, if you're in a relationship with a man who had kids with another woman before you two were a couple, do not keep your man from seeing his kids; allow him to play a significant role in their life. That type of behavior is selfish and inconsiderate on your part and will cause your man to withhold a portion of his love from you.

3. *Emasculate your man.* Remember, a man is going to go where his masculinity is reinforced. When a woman strips her man of his masculinity, she's sending the message that she does not respect him and, ultimately, will lose the support she would have received from him had she not done so.

When you deny your man of his ability to take charge of most situations that affect his family, his growth as a man is severely stifled and his ability to make some of the easiest decisions become difficult for him. As a result, he is left with no significant sense of self-worth and his overall attraction to you suffers severely. This is also the reason why it's important for you to avoid raising your voice to your man, especially while in public. Your man hates a loud-mouthed woman and can't stand being embarrassed by her in public. As a woman, if you feel you must put your man "in-check," make sure it's when no one else is around; ensure that you and he are the only ones who can hear the conversation. Otherwise, he may exhibit defense mechanisms and potentially go off on you once he feels he is left with no other choice. This is because a man doesn't like to be upstaged by his woman, especially in a setting where others can see it; for example at his job, in front of family members, while at dinner, or in front of his friends and colleagues. A key formula for women to keep in mind about men is: Pride + Sensitivity = The Male Ego!

GIVE HIM SPACE

It's important for you to understand that your man appreciates his space. When your man has just gotten home after a long day at work, please take note of the fact that he does not want to be instantly bombarded with the activities going on in your world. Without sounding harsh, your man needs a moment to decompress and evaluate his own day's events before he makes the transition to reestablishing himself as the man in your life and begin hearing what you have to say. This essential decompression right after work is what I call the time your man needs to "get his mind right." It usually takes about fifteen to thirty minutes for your man to get his mind right before he can successfully transition back into the mode of "Hubby," "Daddy," or whatever pet name you may have for him. In some instances, your man can have time to get his mind right during his ride home from work. Unless they're competing with hectic traffic jams on gridlocked highways, most men find their ride home from work to be quite therapeutic, allowing them time to reflect on their day and prepare for a reunion with you and the rest of the family.

When your man has already cleared it with you that he is going out with the fellas, he would prefer for you to not smother him with what I call "electronic space invasion." By constantly communicating with him electronically when he's not around, via text messages, phone calls, etc., you appear extremely insecure and unbalanced to your man and the people he's hanging with. This drives him nuts and it puts him in the awkward position of trying to make excuses for your compulsive behavior. If you contact your man more than five times during every hour he's gone (in a non-emergency situation), your man is going to get extremely frustrated with you, the guys he's hanging with will more than likely ridicule him for being a distraction, and the next time his friends see you they will remember those times you were constantly communicating with him, will give each other a look that says, "Yeah, she's cute, but she is crazy as hell!" As a matter of fact, this reminds me about one of my golfing buddies whose wife called or texted him during every other hole and started off asking him to bring home something from the grocery store while we were on the front nine, then started calling and asking him, "When are you coming home?" or "How much longer will it be before you're finished?" on the back nine. Not only did my golf buddy earn an unflattering nickname for his wife's constant "space invasion" she ended up earning a nickname, not to mention a reputation for being a nag. Don't let your man turn out to be "That guy!"

Although it's important to give your man his proper space, it's equally important to know what constitutes too much space. It's good to have a man who's trustworthy and can be given the benefit of the doubt that he will do the right thing when it comes to other women, especially when you are not around. However, it's important to try not to let your man be without you for long periods of time. What's a long period of time? From the men surveyed, it was determined that an average of forty-five consecutive days is the most reasonable amount of time for a man who honors his relationship with his woman to be without her at one time. I don't mean to imply your man would otherwise cheat on you if his time without you exceeds forty-five days; I'm simply suggesting that this is the approximate timespan in which a man can physically be without his woman before he starts to crave her feminine attention. Also (whenever it's feasible), I would encourage you to occasionally accompany your man on business trips, especially if his business keeps him on the road more than fifteen days per month. As I have mentioned, men are creatures of habit who adapt to nearly any lifestyle once it has become routine to them.

YOUR MAN IS SENSITIVE

According to my e-dictionary, a sensitive person is someone who is 1. Thoughtful and sympathetic; tactful with relation to the feelings of others; and also, 2. Touchy . . . easily offended or annoyed if something is spoken about them or done to them.

With that said, do you think your man is sensitive? Before answering, think back to the times when you've seen how a woman responded to a little boy (younger than four years old) who had fallen down and scraped his knee; then, think of the times you've witnessed how a man responded to a little girl, also younger than four, who had fallen down and scraped her knee. Usually, there is very little variation between the responses. If anything, men typically respond in a more "sensitive" manner than women.

Since about the age of four years old, your man was told, "Little boys shouldn't be cry-babies"; "Be tough, shake it off"; "Walk it off, you'll be okay"; or, better yet, "Man-up boy . . . don't be a little punk (or) sissy!"

Now whether or not any of these statements are right or wrong, as a man and a father of a seven-year-old boy, I understand what is meant by these chauvinistic remarks that are mostly made by men. Fathers want their son to be physically tough, rugged and able to defend himself as years progress towards him becoming a man. Whether a father or a mother, I must contend that I have yet to encounter a parent who had hopes that their child would display homosexual behaviors from day one. However, I have encountered numerous parents who have confirmed that if their son did display such behaviors, they would love him all the same.

Because a macho mindset was embedded in your man at an extremely young age, his reality often left him with no one to turn to when it came to expressing his delicate side because of his fear of being viewed as "soft" or a social misfit. He couldn't talk to his male friends because he didn't want to seem as if he wasn't tough and he felt he couldn't talk to any of his female friends because he didn't want to lose out on the chance of possibly getting laid. As a result, his internal frustration grew and he created masks to hide his touchy-feely side. By the time he became a man, it was difficult for him to express any tender emotion he truly felt inside to his woman because he was rarely ever encouraged to do so. This is why at the beginning of the relationship your man will feel that expressing his vulnerabilities to you will compromise his masculinity. It's not that he doesn't want to tell you how he feels, it's really just because he doesn't know how to express his feelings. Your man is so sensitive that, he wants you to consider him first before you offer anyone else a courteous gesture that he may have possibly wanted (i.e., a piece of chewing gum, the uneaten portion of your meal, taking his plate after he's finished eating, and so forth). Until he deals with and releases his insecurities, it will be hard for him to say the words, "I love you" first. For him, it's more suitable to say, "I love you, too" because that way, he doesn't have to compromise his vulnerable side when responding to such an emotional sentiment.

Your man is sensitive, and this sensitivity will manifest itself in myriad ways. He may shut down and get very quiet, ignore you for a while, develop a stutter, become verbally abusive, or worse, become physically abusive (I'll say it again, Pride + Sensitivity = The Male Ego). Most men take pride in being in control of every situation, and when they feel they've lost control of the situation they tend to get uncomfortable. How your man handles that discomfort, just as he copes with other situations, may vary. It's up to his smart, intuitive woman to notice a change in his habits or behaviors. If for some unfortunate reason, your man becomes physically abusive as a result of his sensitivity, please know that you have far better options to choose from than accepting physical abuse. I'm not trying to sound like a public service announcement, but I do not condone physically abusive relationships (whether the abuser is a woman or a man), and especially if there are children involved.

Because your man is sensitive, he will not share with you every single emotion or thought that exists within his heart and head. One reason for this is because he feels the judgment you would place on him would not be worth the pain and embarrassment he would suffer if he did share these things with you. Also, your man doesn't know how well you would be able to safeguard what he keeps deep in his heart under lock and key. The last thing your man would want you to do with any sensitive information he has shared with you is to throw it back in his face at a later time, or worse, find out you have disclosed his intimate information to someone else. Not to say that your man doesn't trust you overall; it's just that your man may have trust issues with you in this particular area of your relationship. Furthermore, there are some intimate issues that he may not ever be willing to share with you but might possibly want to discuss with his best male friend, or perhaps even another woman. At times, your man will consult another woman in order to try and get a better perspective of understanding you.

Although your man can become quite emotional at times, you will almost never witness his emotional side to the fullest. Rest assured that your man has found a special place where he feels comfortable to be alone and simply cry. Some of the places your man may choose to go and release his emotions could be the bathroom while taking a shower, in his car (especially if he has tinted windows or if he's not in bumper-to-bumper traffic where someone else can see him), or sometimes, while lying in bed in a position turned away from you so you can't see his face. I'm not suggesting your man has these moments often; however, I am suggesting these moments happen far more often than you may imagine. What is he crying about? Past decisions he's made, missing a loved one who has passed away, fear of not having a clear vision of the future, and the stress of making the best decisions for his family. This is the side of your man that he is very mindful about ensuring that most people don't see. By the time your man decides to share the topic with you that had him crying, undoubtedly, his tears would have been long washed away; the fact that he actually had been crying may never even come up.

Before I move on, here's another sensitive nugget that describes your man. Your man does not like to see another man in the same venue wearing the exact same outfit (i.e., suit, designer shirt, or sweater) as he is, regardless of whether he is cool with the other guy or not. If and when that happens, he will make certain to stay on the opposite sides of the room from the other guy who's wearing the same outfit. And for heaven's sake, don't let it be a function where pictures are taken; your man would rather kiss a snaggle-toothed jackass on the mouth before taking a picture with another man with the same outfit as him!

YOU AND YOUR MAN
WHILE WATCHING SPORTS

Your man thinks it is cool for his woman to watch sports games with him, especially if she can talk the language of the game being watched. However, if you can't really talk the language of the game being watched, this is not a major problem for your man. Your man does not mind answering your sport questions periodically, because to him it shows participation on the woman's part, as if she's saying, "Hey, this game is kinda' cool. I'm gonna' ask him a question in order to help me understand this game better!" As a rule of thumb, it is important for you to try not to ask more than two questions every ten minutes or so during the game (for most men, waiting until a commercial break or half-time to ask questions would be perfect), otherwise, more questions would become distracting and could cause him to miss a great portion of the game, similar to how it would be if you were watching your favorite television show.

This is mainly advice to follow when the fellas aren't there to watch the game with your man. A safe rule of thumb for women to go by is that when no more than two of your man's guy friends are there watching the game with him, it's usually safe for you stay and watch it with them. If three or more of the fellas are there to watch the game with your man, and you are the only female in the room, your man would rather you find something else to do in another room or somewhere else, even preferring that you leave the building altogether. This is usually because your man does not have time to monitor both the game and his buddies to ensure they are not trying to get a sneak peek of your body part(s) that's usually not seen when you are out in public. This isn't to say that the same ogling wouldn't happen with just one or two of the fellas around; it's just more likely for your man to have a better chance catching the guy who was looking too hard at you in the first place when there are just a few people in the room.

CLOSING REMARKS

Writing this book has been an amazing experience. I never would have thought that God would have chosen me, a man who was once a lil' skinny kid from Pensacola, Florida, to be given a platform to touch lives in the manner in which He has called me to do. I'm also honored to know that you thought enough of me to read the message that I had to share. I never imagined that the conversations I overheard in San Diego and Washington DC back in August and September of 2009 would have come to this!

I would like to give a special acknowledgement to all of the married women whom I have communicated with over the past couple of years who were looking for answers as they fought to salvage struggling relationships with husbands who just seemed to refuse to honor their wedding vows.

I know those times can be difficult, but I'm a living witness that men can change. I would encourage you to reference 1Peter 3:1-4, which is filled with testaments to a husband's ability to grow. To paraphrase, 1 Peter 3 contends that a husband can change based on his wife's spiritual influence, its wisdom still holds true today: (1) Wives, submit yourselves to your own husbands so that, if any of them do not believe the word, they may be won over without words but by the behavior of their wives; (2) When they see the purity and reverence filling your lives, rejoice at the acknowledgment; (3) Your beauty should not only come from outward adornments, such as elaborate hairstyles and the wearing of gold jewelry or fine clothes; (4) Beauty should come from your inner self, the unfading beauty of a gentle and quiet spirit, which is of greater worth in God's sight.

To me, this is an excellent passage to embrace, because far too often we as humans get in the way of ourselves and end up missing the blessings that were meant for us when we try to do things our way instead of God's way. Now I admit, God's way may not always be the easiest way (or the quickest), but I have yet to witness a time when His way was not the best way, not to mention done with perfect timing! My prayer is that I've provided you with some helpful insight regarding men that you can rightfully apply to your everyday life.

1 Peter 3:7 reads: *Husbands, in the same way be considerate as you live with your wives, and treat*

them with respect as the weaker partner and as heirs with you of the gracious gift of life, so that nothing will hinder your prayers and progress.

To me, this passage suggests that a husband should not take his wife for granted and should assume the responsibilities of maintaining a marriage in which he is respectful to her, honoring her so that he does not compromise the success and joy intended for him and his family. Personally, I have never encountered anyone or anything suggesting marriage would be easy. Therefore, it's vitally important that you don't intentionally do anything that will hinder you and your spouse's progress.

There's one other pitfall every woman should avoid in her relationships: Do not allow your relationship with your man to determine your self-worth! I encourage you to not become the woman who measures her self-fulfillment in life entirely upon her man's opinion of her. If so, chances are you will be left totally lost in the event the relationship does not work out. I am not suggesting that you should not give it your all while in a relationship; I am merely warning you not to let your identity be solely defined by your role as your man's woman. It's extremely important for women to establish an identity beyond the title of "wife," "girlfriend," "baby's mama," and, especially, the "woman on the side."

I say this because there are so many instances where a woman puts her life's dreams and goals completely aside in order for her man to see his dreams and goals through. Now, granted, this is truly a noble sacrifice for the women who do this; however, with equitable family goals in place, both you and your man should be able to achieve personal success in a manner that will benefit you as a couple. Simply put, I encourage all women to pursue their goals of becoming a doctor, registered nurse, cosmetologist, teacher, wedding planner, business owner, etc., because when these dreams are left unfulfilled, all kinds of resentments towards themselves and the people around them are created. *Do not* make your man your god, because if and when you do, that will mark the beginning of your disappointments in life. Instead, direct your attention towards your Creator and ask for proper guidance when seeking your heart's desires. Of course, anything worth having will require endurance, discipline, and sacrifice to attain; however, do not sell yourself short by thinking you lack the time or abilities to achieve your goals.

Lastly, there's an element of good and bad that dwells within all of us. For the sake of labeling, I will refer to the bad as "The Enemy." The enemy is not a he or a she—it's more like a *force* or a *movement*; therefore, I refer to the enemy as an "it." The enemy's goal is to kill, steal, and destroy. This goal could be targeted towards destroying your will to succeed in your marriage, to be happy, to feel secure within yourself, and, most notably, destroy your will to live. As long as the enemy feels threatened by whatever good you and your man can accomplish by working together as a team, it will do all it can to try and drive a wedge between you and your man. The enemy understands that if it can stir up feelings of distrust, insecurities, or thoughts or acts of infidelity, the chance of destroying you and your man's goal of having a positive relationship increases.

In order to avoid being sucked into the enemy's scheme, it's important for you and your man to communicate with one another about whatever it is you feel is creating that wedge. Otherwise, a lot of negative reactions could emerge as a result of one not letting the other know what's really going on.

ASK THE ASCOT AUTHOR ...

1. Ms. Lady from South Florida . . . *Hello Mr. Ascot Author, I am sorry to say that two years ago I cheated on my husband with another man and I have spent everyday since then trying to make it up to him and our family in an effort to make things right. In fact, for the past year, I have been reading my bible more in an attempt to get my life right. As expected, some days are better than others between my husband and me, yet I was confident that he and I were moving forward in a positive direction regarding the recovery of our marriage. Unfortunately, for the past four months, he has become very "distant" towards me, has been staying out late nights and coming home long enough to shower and change his clothes before he heads back out the door to go to work. I am convinced he is involved with another woman because he is not good at "covering his tracks." I have considered leaving him, but my kids need their father; plus, I feel I am only getting what I deserve because of my infidelity two years ago. What should I do?*

Ascot Author: Ms. Lady . . . I am sorry to hear that the relationship between you and your husband is not the most amicable right now. I commend you for realizing the error of your ways two years ago and recommitting yourself to being an honorable wife. I, too, know what it is like to give in to one's own selfish desires and not consider the negative affects my actions would have on my family. It sounds to me that your husband may be suffering from internal conflict right now. He loves you, but your betrayal of his trust in you makes it hard for him to simply forgive you. It took him a long time to get to the level of trust that he once had for you, and now he's left to try to start all over at rebuilding it again. If so, he is not thinking clearly about the damage he is causing—not only to himself, but also to the people who love him. To put it frankly, your husband is what I call "Damaged Goods." Damaged goods is the mentality most men adopt once they have been betrayed by a woman. When you mix a man's pride with his sensitivity, you get an ego as a result (and egos hardly ever come in small packages). When a man's ego gets bruised, he reacts; the way he reacts is not the same for every man. Nonetheless, his reaction will be an effort to heal the bruised ego he has suffered. My advice for you (as his wife) would be to surround yourself around spiritual women of God who have experienced what you are experiencing right now and seek their counsel. Typically, these types of spiritual women are older than you and understand the importance of marriage's sanctity. I would also advise for you to continue to do what is asked of you as a Proverbs 31:10-31 woman. Afterwards, have a rational, heart-to-heart talk with your husband and let him know that you are well aware of his infidelity and have decided to let God handle it because he will do a job far better than you; besides, if you were to handle the situation the way you wanted to, you would more than likely end up in up in some serious legal trouble. You must realize your kids deserve better than being without both parents. Politely end the conversation and go about your duties as a wife and mother. Treat your husband with kindness, greet him with a smile, start (or continue) an exercise/fitness regimen, continue to keep up your appearance, and avoid any further confrontations with him if possible. Before long, your man will see the change in you, your appearance, and your behavior, and he will begin to ask you questions. Let your man know that you have vowed to put your faith in things that are not seen as if they were already there. In time, God will intervene on your behalf and give signs that will show you what's best for you and your children. Keep in mind that this will only happen in your favor if you conduct yourself in a manner that is pleasing to God. Otherwise, your situation will be reduced to a marriage in which both husband and wife are doing foolish things to hurt one another even though, their children are the ones who end up getting hurt the most. Be blessed, Ms. Lady, and I pray for restoration within your family's household.

(2) Ms. Lady from Cleveland, Ohio . . . *Dear Mr. Ascot Author, what was the most consistent thing you learned about men after conducting your surveys?* The most consistent thing that I learned after conducting my survey is that men are sensitive! I never would have guessed that some of the toughest men I met while collecting my data were also some of the most sensitive. I'm not saying this in a negative way, but I must admit that I was delightfully surprised to have so many men share some of their most vulnerable experiences with me. Not accounting for all, but a lot of the tougher guys I surveyed (i.e., the ones known for knocking people out and appearing to be the meanest), were the ones who were the most sensitive.

Men don't like to have their feelings hurt and, unlike women, it's usually unbecoming for a man to say, "You hurt my feelings when you said [or did] that" to another man if he hasn't been friends with him for many years. Even then, it's still difficult for a man to express to someone else in words that his feelings have been hurt; he usually responds with some type of loud or aggressive behavior in order to soothe the feeling of a bruised ego.

(3) Mr. Baltimore, Maryland . . . *Dear Mr. Ascot, my wife and I have been together for a total of 15 years. Without question, I'm still in love with her; however, I*

find myself not being sexually interested in her like I used to be. Yes, she has gained a little weight, but I still find her attractive. What do you feel is the best way for me to tell my wife that we need to spice up our sex life without me getting her upset?

Mr. Baltimore, this issue can turn into a serious problem if you're not careful. My advice would be for you to be open and honest with your wife; however, I say this with reservations. Because you feel this way about your wife, you can more than likely be certain that she has already sensed your sexual disinterest in her soon after you started feeling that way (it's a sixth sense that she has as a woman). Perhaps you could interest your wife in having an affair with you (similar to what was suggested in the movie *Little Fockers*). Instead of the typical way you two normally propose sex to one another, spice it up by asking her to wear a different hairstyle. If she has long hair, ask her to change it up and wear a stylish, short hairdo. If her hair is naturally brown or brunette, pay for her to get it highlighted or changed to another color that compliments her looks. You could also make plans for you and she to have sex in a place other than where you two normally meet (i.e., arrange to meet on the beach, at a hotel, on an office desk, or in the bathroom of a large social gathering). Between your wife wearing various hairstyles and you two having sex in unusual places, chances are it will create the seductive illusion of having sex with someone other than the wife you have come to know. Remember, nothing is sexually defiled between husband and wife as long as you two are both in agreement (keep it legal)!

CONTACT PAGE

"Like" me now on fb: The Ascot Author

Follow me on Twitter: theascotauthor

For relationship questions/comments or to schedule a group seminar, send your requests to: dariusdonte@theascotauthor.com

PHOTO GALLERY

Special thanks to:

Mr. V-Bland

Mr D-R-E

Mr. J. "Rob" Smith

Mr. and Mrs. Darius Donte'

Cheers Everyone!

Darius Donte'